BACON
everything

83
PRESS®

BACON
everything

**BACON
MAKES
EVERYTHING
BETTER!**

83 Press
1900 International Park Drive, Suite 50
Birmingham, Alabama 35243
83press.com

ISBN: 978-1-940772-93-6
Printed in China

Contents

BACON BASICS

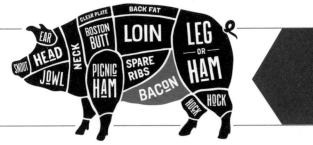

Whether you like it thin and crispy or hearty and thick-cut, everyone loves a good slice of bacon.

WANT CRISPIER BACON?

Select a thinner cut and remove fat as it accumulates during the cooking process.

COLD BACON, COLD PAN

Starting in a cold pan gives the bacon more time to render fat and cook evenly.

NEED TO FEED A CROWD?

Line a large baking sheet with foil; place bacon in an even layer. Bake at 400° until crisp, about 20 minutes.

BACON FAT 101

In the South, we love bacon fat as much as we love bacon itself. But a lot of folks don't realize how versatile this ingredient really is. Follow these tips to ensure no drop of this liquid gold goes to waste.

DEDICATE A JAR

It's important to have a heatproof container for bacon fat. Don't add any other type of grease to it. Once your bacon fat has cooled slightly, add it to the container and screw the lid on tight.

KEEP IN THE FRIDGE

Bacon fat has traditionally been stored on the counter or stovetop, but it's best to keep it in the refrigerator. Cold bacon grease is the consistency of shortening, making it a cinch to spoon out a little bit for recipes.

FREEZE EXTRA FAT

When you have a full jar of bacon fat, it can be sealed and frozen. Then you can start another jar in the refrigerator. It never hurts to have extra bacon fat on hand, and it lasts indefinitely in the freezer when well covered.

THICK-CUT

Our choice for cooking until crisp and serving alongside eggs and other foods, thick-cut bacon slices are typically between ⅛-inch and ¼-inch thickness and produce a good amount of drippings when cooked.

REGULAR

The standard for sliced bacon, it cooks up thin and crispy for that melt-in-your-mouth texture. Regular bacon slices are great for crumbling to use as a topping or for adding to baked goods.

CENTER-CUT

This cut of bacon has the fat trimmed off both sides. These slices are from the center of the slab. Center-cut bacon is generally meatier than regular or thick-cut and produces less drippings when cooked.

SLAB

A bacon slab is the whole piece of cured pork belly before it's sliced. It provides flexibility when cutting, whether in cubes, thin strips, or extra-thick slices. Cubing slab bacon is ideal for browning and using as a seasoning meat.

CANADIAN

Cured in a similar fashion to American bacon, Canadian bacon is made from pork loin, not pork belly. It's leaner but still packs a lot of flavor and is a good choice for using in casseroles and on sandwiches.

Wrapped

WITH

BACON

Starters, sides, and main dishes
that prove everything is better
wrapped with bacon

BACON-JALAPEÑO MEAT LOAF

12 slices thick-cut bacon, divided
2 pounds ground sirloin
2 large eggs, lightly beaten
2 cloves garlic, minced
1 jalapeño pepper, seeded and minced
2/3 cup panko (Japanese bread crumbs)
1/2 cup chopped green onion
6 tablespoons ketchup, divided
2 tablespoons pepper sauce
8 teaspoons Worcestershire sauce, divided
2 teaspoons Dijon mustard
1 teaspoon kosher salt
1/2 teaspoon ground black pepper
1/4 cup firmly packed light brown sugar
1/2 cup pickled jalapeño slices

1. Preheat oven to 350°.

2. In a 12-inch cast-iron skillet, cook 8 slices bacon over medium heat until crisp. Remove bacon, and let drain on paper towels. Let cool; crumble bacon. Pour off drippings from skillet.

3. In a large bowl, gently stir together beef, eggs, garlic, minced jalapeño, bread crumbs, green onion, 2 tablespoons ketchup, pepper sauce, 6 teaspoons Worcestershire, mustard, salt, pepper, and crumbled bacon until combined. Transfer meat mixture to skillet, and shape into a rectangle. Cut remaining 4 slices bacon in half crosswise; place on top of meat loaf.

4. In a small bowl, stir together brown sugar, remaining 4 tablespoons ketchup, and remaining 2 teaspoons Worcestershire. Brush half of mixture onto bacon; top with pickled jalapeño slices.

5. Bake for 45 minutes. Brush remaining glaze onto meat loaf. Bake until a meat thermometer inserted in center registers 165°, about 30 minutes more. Broil until bacon is crisp, 2 to 3 minutes, if desired. Let stand for 10 minutes before slicing.

KITCHEN TIP

It's important to use ground sirloin or lean ground beef in this meat loaf so that, with the addition of bacon, your final dish isn't too fatty or greasy.

BACON-WRAPPED STEAKS WITH BACON-THYME BUTTER

Makes 4 servings

6   slices bacon, divided
½   cup unsalted butter,
     softened
2   teaspoons finely chopped
     fresh thyme
1½   teaspoons kosher salt,
     divided
4   (1½-inch-thick) beef
     tenderloin fillets
1   teaspoon ground black
     pepper
Garnish: fresh thyme

1. In a 10-inch cast-iron skillet, cook 2 slices bacon over medium heat until crisp, about 5 minutes. Remove bacon, and let drain on paper towels; finely chop bacon. Pour off drippings from skillet; reserve.

2. In a small bowl, stir together butter, 1 teaspoon reserved bacon drippings, thyme, ½ teaspoon salt, and chopped bacon until well combined. Transfer butter mixture to a sheet of parchment or wax paper. Tightly roll into a log, and twist ends to secure. Freeze until solid, about 30 minutes.

3. Wrap 1 slice bacon around sides of each fillet; secure with wooden picks. Sprinkle pepper and remaining 1 teaspoon salt onto fillets.

4. In same skillet, heat 3 teaspoons reserved bacon drippings over medium-high heat. Place fillets in skillet, bacon side down. Cook, turning occasionally, until bacon is browned and crisp. Place steaks flat in skillet; cook for about 5 minutes per side for medium-rare or to desired degree of doneness is reached. Top fillets with butter mixture; let stand for 5 minutes. Remove picks before serving. Garnish with thyme, if desired.

KITCHEN TIP

The bacon-thyme butter is also delicious spread onto warm bread, dolloped onto baked potatoes, or stirred into grits.

BACON-WRAPPED CHICKEN BREASTS WITH BRUSSELS SPROUTS

Makes 6 servings

1¼ teaspoons kosher salt, divided
½ teaspoon ground black pepper
6 boneless skinless chicken breasts
12 slices center-cut bacon
¾ pound Brussels sprouts, trimmed and halved
2 tablespoons water
1 tablespoon canola oil
¼ teaspoon garlic powder
½ cup dry white wine
¾ cup heavy whipping cream
2 tablespoons Dijon mustard

1. Preheat oven to 400°.
2. Sprinkle 1 teaspoon salt and pepper all over chicken. Tightly wrap 2 pieces of bacon around each chicken breast; secure with wooden picks.
3. In a microwave-safe dish, combine Brussels sprouts and 2 tablespoons water. Cover with plastic wrap, leaving one corner of dish uncovered. Microwave on high for 2 minutes. Carefully uncover; drain well.
4. In a 12-inch cast-iron skillet, heat oil over medium-high heat. Add Brussels sprouts, garlic powder, and remaining ¼ teaspoon salt; cook, stirring occasionally, until lightly browned, 4 to 5 minutes. Remove sprouts from skillet.
5. Add chicken to skillet; cook over medium heat until bacon is browned, 5 to 6 minutes per side. Transfer skillet to oven.
6. Bake for 20 minutes. Remove chicken from skillet, reserving 2 tablespoons drippings in skillet.
7. Heat skillet over medium-high heat. Stir in wine. In a small bowl, whisk together cream and mustard; whisk into wine in skillet. Cook until thickened, 2 to 3 minutes. Return chicken and Brussels sprouts to skillet; cook until heated through. Remove picks before serving.

APPLE AND COLLARDS STUFFED PORK LOIN

3   tablespoons bacon drippings or canola oil
1   cup diced yellow onion
1   tablespoon minced garlic
1   (1-pound) bag chopped stemmed collard greens
1   cup apple cider
2   cups diced Pink Lady apple (about 2 large apples)
2   teaspoons kosher salt, divided
1   teaspoon minced fresh sage
¼   teaspoon chopped fresh thyme
¼   teaspoon ground black pepper, divided
⅛   teaspoon lemon zest
1   (3-pound) boneless pork loin, trimmed
1   (16-ounce) package bacon
6   shallots
5   small Gala apples, halved
Garnish: fresh sage

1. In a large Dutch oven, heat drippings or oil over medium heat. Add onion and garlic; cook, stirring occasionally, until softened, about 6 minutes.
2. Stir in greens in batches; cook until wilted. Stir in cider; cover and cook until greens are tender, about 30 minutes.
3. Stir Pink Lady apples, 1½ teaspoons salt, sage, thyme, ⅛ teaspoon pepper, and zest into greens. Cook, uncovered, until liquid has evaporated and apples are just tender, about 5 minutes. Remove from heat; let mixture cool to room temperature.
4. Preheat oven to 400°. Place a wire rack in a large roasting pan.
5. Butterfly and flatten pork loin to ¼-inch thickness. Sprinkle remaining ½ teaspoon salt and remaining ⅛ teaspoon pepper onto pork. Spread greens mixture onto pork, leaving a 1-inch border on all sides. Tightly roll up pork loin and filling into a log.
6. Wrap bacon slices around pork to fully cover, overlapping slices as needed. Tie pork at 1-inch intervals with kitchen string. Place pork in prepared pan.
7. Bake for 30 minutes. Add shallots and Gala apples to pan around pork. Bake until a meat thermometer inserted in center of pork registers 130° to 135°, about 20 minutes more. Let stand for 10 minutes before slicing. Garnish with sage, if desired.

SPICY MAPLE-GLAZED BACON-WRAPPED CARROTS

Makes 6 to 8 servings

2   pounds carrots, trimmed
     and peeled
1   (16-ounce) package bacon
¼   cup maple syrup
½   teaspoon kosher salt
¼   teaspoon crushed red pepper
⅛   teaspoon ground black pepper

1. Preheat oven to 400°. Line a large rimmed baking sheet with foil.
2. Wrap each carrot with bacon. Place on prepared pan. Bake for 40 minutes.
3. In a small bowl, whisk together maple syrup, salt, and peppers. Brush onto carrots; bake until bacon is crisp and carrots are tender, about 15 minutes more.

KITCHEN TIP

Cane or sorghum syrup can be substituted for maple syrup.

BACON-WRAPPED PORK WITH ROASTED VEGETABLES

Makes 4 to 6 servings

4   cloves garlic, grated
1½   tablespoons chopped
     fresh rosemary
1   tablespoon fennel
     seeds, crushed
1½   teaspoons kosher salt
1   teaspoon crushed
     red pepper
1   teaspoon lemon zest
2   pounds Brussels sprouts,
     trimmed and halved
2   (8-ounce) packages
     baby carrots
6   shallots, halved
1   (1½-pound) pork
     tenderloin
8   slices bacon
3   teaspoons olive oil,
     divided

1. Preheat oven to 425°.

2. In a small bowl, stir together garlic, rosemary, fennel seeds, salt, red pepper, and zest. In a large bowl, stir together Brussels sprouts, carrots, shallots, and 1 tablespoon garlic mixture.

3. Rub remaining garlic mixture onto pork. Wrap bacon slices around pork, overlapping slices slightly.

4. In a 12-inch cast-iron skillet, heat 1½ teaspoons oil over medium-high heat. Add pork; cook until browned on all sides, 1 to 2 minutes per side. Add vegetables to pan around pork; drizzle remaining 1½ teaspoons oil onto vegetables.

5. Bake until a meat thermometer inserted in center of pork registers 140° and vegetables are tender, about 25 minutes. Let stand for 10 minutes before slicing.

BACON-WRAPPED SHRIMP AND SCALLOPS

Makes 6 to 8 servings

1 pound cherrywood-smoked bacon, slices halved lengthwise and crosswise

1 pound extra-large fresh shrimp, peeled and deveined (tails left on)

1 pound large fresh scallops, patted dry

½ cup red pepper jelly

6 tablespoons olive oil

2 teaspoon kosher salt

1 teaspoon ground black pepper

1. Wrap 1 piece of bacon around each shrimp; secure with wooden picks.

2. Wrap 1 piece of bacon around sides of each scallop; secure with wooden picks.

3. In a small bowl, whisk together pepper jelly, oil, salt, and pepper.

4. Heat a 12-inch cast-iron skillet over medium-high heat. Place wrapped shrimp in an even layer in pan. Cook until golden brown, about 2 minutes; turn.

5. Brush pepper jelly mixture onto shrimp; cook until firm to the touch, about 2 minutes. Remove from skillet; wipe skillet clean.

6. Heat same skillet over medium-high heat. Place wrapped scallops in even layer in pan. Cook until golden brown, about 3 minutes; turn. Brush pepper jelly mixture onto scallops; cook until firm to the touch, about 3 minutes. Remove picks before serving.

KITCHEN TIP

Shrimp is often sold by the count rather than size. Extra-large shrimp generally are 26–30, which means that 26 to 30 shrimp weigh approximately 1 pound. Look for sea scallops, which are large, for this recipe; bay scallops are small and not suitable for this dish.

CHEESY BACON BREADSTICKS

1 tablespoon firmly packed light brown sugar
¾ teaspoon chili powder
⅛ teaspoon onion powder
½ (17.3-ounce) package frozen puff pastry, thawed according to package directions
¼ cup shredded sharp Cheddar cheese
6 slices bacon, halved lengthwise
1 large egg
1 teaspoon water

1. Preheat oven to 400°. Line a large rimmed baking sheet with foil. Place a wire rack on prepared pan; spray rack with cooking spray.

2. In a small bowl, whisk together brown sugar, chili powder, and onion powder.

3. On a lightly floured surface, unfold puff pastry sheet; roll into a 12x10-inch rectangle. Sprinkle cheese and half of brown sugar mixture onto bottom half of short side of pastry. Fold top half of pastry onto filling; roll pastry into a 12x10-inch rectangle. Cut dough into 10 (12-inch-long) strips.

4. Place one piece of bacon on each pastry strip; twist together. Place on prepared rack.

5. In a small bowl, whisk together egg and 1 teaspoon water; lightly brush onto twists. Sprinkle with remaining brown sugar mixture.

6. Bake until golden brown, 12 to 15 minutes. Let cool on pan for 5 minutes before serving.

BACON-WRAPPED ASPARAGUS AND GREEN BEAN BUNDLES

5   teaspoons kosher salt, divided
1   pound fresh green beans, trimmed
2   pounds fresh asparagus, trimmed
1   (16-ounce) package peppered bacon, slices halved crosswise
3   slices thick-cut bacon, finely chopped
2½ tablespoons sherry vinegar
1   tablespoon whole-grain mustard
1   teaspoon chopped fresh thyme

1. Fill a small Dutch oven halfway with water and 3 teaspoons salt; bring to a boil over high heat. Add green beans; cook until crisp-tender, about 3 minutes. Drain beans, and rinse under cold water. Drain well; pat dry with paper towels.

2. Wrap bundles of 8 to 10 green beans with bacon, tying in a knot. Wrap bundles of 5 to 6 asparagus with bacon, trimming ends; secure with wooden picks.

3. Heat a 12-inch cast-iron skillet over medium-high heat. Place green bean bundles in batches in an even layer in pan; sprinkle with 1 teaspoon salt. Cook until bacon is crisp, about 2 minutes per side. Remove from skillet; keep warm. Pour off drippings in skillet.

4. In same skillet, place asparagus bundles in batches in an even layer; sprinkle with remaining 1 teaspoon salt. Cook until bacon is crisp and asparagus is tender, about 2 minutes per side. Pour off drippings in skillet. Remove picks from asparagus bundles. Return green bean bundles to skillet with asparagus bundles.

5. Meanwhile, in a medium cast-iron skillet, cook chopped bacon over medium-high heat until crisp, about 6 minutes. Remove from heat; stir in vinegar, mustard, and thyme. Drizzle onto vegetable bundles; serve immediately.

BACON-WRAPPED CHICKEN THIGHS

1 teaspoon kosher salt
½ teaspoon ground black pepper
8 boneless skinless chicken thighs
8 slices thick-cut bacon
2 small red onions, cut into wedges
3 cloves garlic, crushed
1 tablespoon molasses
1 teaspoon whole-grain mustard
2 tablespoons all-purpose flour
1½ cups heavy whipping cream
1 tablespoon chopped fresh thyme
Garnish: fresh thyme

1. Preheat oven to 350°.
2. Sprinkle salt and pepper all over chicken. Tightly wrap one piece of bacon around each chicken thigh. Tuck ends of bacon under to secure.
3. Heat a 12-inch cast-iron skillet over medium-high heat. Add chicken; cook, turning twice, until bacon begins to crisp. Add onion and garlic; cook until onion is almost tender, about 4 minutes. In a small bowl, whisk together molasses and mustard; brush onto chicken.
4. Bake until a meat thermometer inserted in thickest portion registers 165°, about 20 minutes. Remove chicken, onion, and garlic from skillet, reserving ¼ cup drippings in skillet.
5. Heat skillet over medium heat. Whisk in flour until smooth; cook until bubbly, about 1 minute. Reduce heat to low; gradually whisk in cream until smooth; whisk in thyme. Return chicken, onion, and garlic to skillet; cook until heated through. Garnish with thyme, if desired.

topped

WITH

BACON

A sprinkle of salty, crispy bacon
takes every dish over the top

CREAMY GARLIC BACON PORK CHOPS

2   teaspoons kosher salt, divided
1   teaspoon ground black
    pepper, divided
4   (8-ounce) bone-in pork chops
6   slices thick-cut bacon,
    chopped
1   small yellow onion, thinly
    sliced
4   cloves garlic, minced
1½ teaspoons chopped fresh
    rosemary
½   cup dry white wine
1½ cups heavy whipping cream
2   tablespoons Dijon mustard
½   cup shredded Parmesan
    cheese
Garnish: chopped fresh rosemary

1. Sprinkle 1½ teaspoons salt and ½ teaspoon pepper all over pork chops. Let stand at room temperature for 15 minutes.

2. In a 12-inch cast-iron skillet, cook bacon over medium-high heat, stirring occasionally, until crisp, 10 to 12 minutes. Remove using a slotted spoon, and let drain on paper towels, reserving 2 tablespoons drippings in skillet.

3. Add pork chops to drippings in skillet; cook over medium heat until browned, about 3 minutes per side. Remove from pan.

4. Add onion; cook, stirring occasionally, until tender, about 5 minutes. Stir in garlic and rosemary; cook until fragrant, about 1 minute. Stir in white wine; cook until reduced by half, about 1 minute. Stir in cream, mustard, remaining ½ teaspoon salt, and remaining ½ teaspoon pepper; cook, stirring occasionally, until slightly thickened, about 3 minutes. Whisk in cheese until smooth.

5. Return pork chops to skillet; continue until an instant-read thermometer inserted in chops registers 150° and sauce is thickened, about 10 minutes. Top with bacon before serving. Garnish with rosemary, if desired.

SAVORY SWEET POTATO CASSEROLE

6   slices bacon, chopped
1   large yellow onion, thinly sliced (about 3 cups)
1   teaspoon chopped fresh thyme
1   teaspoon chopped fresh rosemary
6   cups mashed cooked sweet potatoes (about 4 large potatoes)
1½ cups shredded Gruyère cheese, divided
½   cup heavy whipping cream
¼   cup unsalted butter, melted
1   large egg, lightly beaten
1½ teaspoons kosher salt
¼   teaspoon ground black pepper
Garnish: fresh rosemary

1. Preheat oven to 350°. Spray a 2-quart baking dish with cooking spray.

2. In a large skillet, cook bacon over medium heat until crisp, about 8 minutes. Remove bacon using a slotted spoon, and let drain on paper towels, reserving 1 tablespoon drippings in skillet.

3. Add onion to drippings in skillet; cook, stirring frequently, until golden brown, about 30 minutes. Stir in thyme and rosemary. Remove from heat.

4. In a large bowl, stir together onion mixture, sweet potato, 1 cup cheese, cream, melted butter, egg, salt, and pepper. Spoon into prepared pan.

5. Bake until heated through, about 30 minutes. Top with remaining ½ cup cheese; bake until melted, about 10 minutes more. Top with bacon before serving. Garnish with rosemary, if desired.

KITCHEN TIP

This casserole can be assembled through step 4, covered, and refrigerated overnight. Uncover and let stand at room temperature for 30 minutes before baking as directed.

BACON MAC AND CHEESE PIE

Makes 1 (9-inch) pie

1   (14.1-ounce) package
     refrigerated piecrusts
3   tablespoons melted bacon
     drippings, divided
1½   tablespoons all-purpose
     flour
½   teaspoon kosher salt
¼   teaspoon ground black
     pepper
1⅓   cups whole milk
1   large egg yolk, lightly
     beaten
¾   cup shredded sharp
     Cheddar cheese, divided
½   cup shredded fontina
     cheese
1   cup small elbow macaroni,
     cooked according to
     package directions
1   cup crumbled cooked
     bacon, divided
¼   cup chopped green onion
½   cup panko (Japanese
     bread crumbs)

1. Preheat oven to 450°.
2. On a lightly floured surface, unroll 1 piecrust. Lightly brush with water, and place remaining crust on top; roll layers together. Transfer to 9-inch pie plate, pressing into bottom and up sides. Fold edges under, and crimp as desired. Prick bottom and sides of crust with a fork. Cover edges of crust with foil.
3. Bake on lowest rack until bottom of crust begins to brown, about 10 minutes. Remove from oven, and let cool completely. Reduce oven temperature to 375°.
4. In a medium saucepan, heat 2 tablespoons bacon drippings over medium heat. Whisk in flour, salt, and pepper; cook for 1 minute. Gradually whisk in milk until smooth; bring to a low boil. Remove from heat.
5. In a medium bowl, gradually whisk half of milk mixture into egg yolk in a slow, steady stream. Whisk egg mixture into remaining milk mixture in saucepan. Cook over medium-low heat, whisking constantly, until bubbly, about 2 minutes. Remove from heat.
6. Whisk ½ cup Cheddar and fontina into milk mixture until melted. Stir in cooked pasta, ¾ cup bacon, and green onion. Spread pasta mixture into prepared crust.
7. In a small bowl, stir together bread crumbs, remaining ¼ cup Cheddar, remaining ¼ cup bacon, and remaining 1 tablespoon bacon drippings. Sprinkle onto pasta.
8. Bake until golden brown and bubbly, about 20 minutes. Let stand for 10 minutes before serving.

SMASHED RED POTATOES WITH BACON

1   (28-ounce) bag baby
    red potatoes
4   teaspoons kosher salt,
    divided
6   slices applewood-smoked
    bacon, chopped
6   cloves garlic, crushed
¼   cup fresh rosemary sprigs
½   teaspoon ground black
    pepper, divided

1. In a large Dutch oven, bring potatoes, 3 teaspoons salt, and water to cover to a boil over medium-high heat. Cook until tender, 15 to 20 minutes; drain well.

2. In a 12-inch cast-iron skillet, cook bacon over medium-high heat, stirring occasionally, until crisp, about 8 minutes. Remove bacon using a slotted spoon, and let drain on paper towels, reserving drippings in skillet.

3. Add half of potatoes, half of garlic, half of rosemary, ½ teaspoon salt, and ¼ teaspoon pepper to drippings in skillet. Using the back of a spoon, smash potatoes. Cook over medium heat until potatoes are browned and crisp, about 5 minutes. Remove from skillet.

4. Repeat procedure with remaining potatoes, garlic, rosemary, remaining ½ teaspoon salt, and remaining ¼ teaspoon pepper. Return all potaotes to skillet; top with bacon before serving.

SKILLET CABBAGE WITH BACON

6   slices thick-cut bacon, chopped
½   red onion, thiny sliced
1   teaspoon fennel seeds, crushed
1   small head green cabbage, cut into 6 wedges (about 2 pounds)
3   tablespoons apple cider vinegar
1   teaspoon kosher salt

1. In a 12-inch cast-iron skillet, cook bacon over medium heat until crisp. Remove bacon using a slotted spoon, and let drain on paper towels, reserving drippings in skillet.

2. Add onion and fennel seeds to pan; cook, stirring occasionally, until lightly browned, 2 to 3 minutes. Remove onion using a slotted spoon. Add cabbage to pan; cook until browned, about 5 minutes.

3. Turn cabbage; return onion to pan, and add vinegar. Cook until softened, about 8 minutes. Turn cabbage; sprinkle with salt, and top with bacon.

KITCHEN TIP

Don't remove the core of the cabbage; it will help keep the wedges from falling apart as they cook.

BACON-TOPPED FRIES WITH GRAVY

3 pounds russet potatoes, peeled and cut into ¼-inch-thick sticks
6 slices bacon, chopped
¼ cup all-purpose flour
¾ teaspoon kosher salt, divided
¼ teaspoon ground black pepper
2 cups low-sodium beef broth
2 sprigs fresh thyme
Vegetable oil, for frying
Cheese curds, to serve
Garnish: chopped fresh parsley

1. In a large bowl, combine cut potatoes and cold water to cover. Let stand for 30 minutes to 1 hour. Drain well, and pat dry.
2. In a large cast-iron skillet, cook bacon over medium-high heat until crisp, about 8 minutes. Remove bacon using a slotted spoon, and let drain on paper towels, reserving drippings in skillet.
3. Whisk flour, ¼ teaspoon salt, and pepper into drippings in skillet; cook over medium heat, whisking constantly, until smooth, about 5 minutes. Gradually whisk in broth until smooth. Add thyme; cook, whisking frequently, until thickened, about 10 minutes. Discard thyme; keep gravy warm over very low heat.
4. In a large Dutch oven, pour oil to a depth of 4 inches, and heat over medium heat until a deep-fry thermometer registers 325°.
5. Fry potatoes in batches until lightly browned, 3 to 4 minutes. Remove from oil, and let drain on paper towels. Increase oil temperature to 375°. Fry potatoes again in batches until golden brown and crisp, 2 to 3 minutes. Remove from oil, and let drain on paper towels. Sprinkle remaining ½ teaspoon salt onto fries. Top fries with, gravy, cheese curds, and bacon. Garnish with parsley, if desired. Serve immediately.

GREENS AND BACON PULL-APART DIP

4 slices bacon, finely chopped
¼ cup finely chopped yellow onion
5 cups chopped fresh turnip greens
½ (8-ounce) package cream cheese, softened
½ cup sour cream
½ cup shredded sharp white Cheddar cheese, divided
6 tablespoons mayonnaise
¼ cup grated Parmesan cheese
¼ teaspoon kosher salt
¼ teaspoon garlic powder
¼ teaspoon ground red pepper
⅛ teaspoon ground cumin
1 (11-ounce) can refrigerated breadsticks*

1. Preheat oven to 375°.
2. In a 10-inch cast-iron skillet, cook bacon over medium heat until crisp. Remove bacon using a slotted spoon, and let drain on paper towels, reserving 2 tablespoons drippings in skillet.
3. To skillet, add onion; cook over medium-high heat until softened, about 2 minutes. Add greens to skillet; cook until wilted, about 4 minutes.
4. In a medium bowl, stir together greens mixture, cream cheese, sour cream, ¼ cup Cheddar, mayonnaise, Parmesan, salt, garlic powder, red pepper, and cumin.
5. On a lightly floured surface, unroll dough, and separate into 12 pieces. Roll each into a spiral; pinch seams to seal. Place rolls around edge of skillet, seam side facing out. Spoon dip in center of skillet.
6. Bake until bread is golden brown and dip is bubbly, about 24 minutes, covering with foil during last 5 minutes of baking to prevent dip from drying out.
7. Uncover dip; sprinkle with remaining ¼ cup Cheddar and bacon. Bake until cheese is melted, about 3 minutes more. Let stand for 10 minutes before serving.

We used Pillsbury Original Breadsticks.

MAC AND CHEESE WITH BACON AND BRUSSELS SPROUTS

1   **pound Brussels sprouts, stemmed and halved**
1   **tablespoon olive oil**
6   **slices bacon, chopped**
½   **cup diced yellow onion**
2   **cloves garlic, minced**
¼   **cup all-purpose flour**
2½   **cups whole milk**
1   **cup grated Parmesan cheese**
1   **cup shredded sharp white Cheddar cheese**
2   **teaspoons kosher salt**
1   **teaspoon Dijon mustard**
¼   **teaspoon crushed red pepper**
8   **ounces bow tie pasta, cooked according to package directions**

1. Preheat oven to 425°. Line a rimmed baking sheet with parchment paper.

2. Toss together Brussels sprouts and oil on prepared pan; arrange in a single layer.

3. Bake until Brussels sprouts are lightly browned, about 15 minutes.

4. In a 10-inch cast-iron skillet, cook bacon over medium heat until crisp, about 8 minutes. Remove bacon using a slotted spoon, and let drain on paper towels, reserving 4 tablespoons drippings in skillet.

5. Add onion and garlic to drippings in skillet; cook, stirring frequently, until softened, about 3 minutes. Whisk in flour; cook, whisking constantly, for 1 minute. Gradually whisk in milk until smooth; cook, whisking constantly, until mixture thickens, about 5 minutes. Remove from heat; stir in cheeses, salt, mustard, and red pepper until smooth. Stir in cooked pasta and Brussels sprouts; top with bacon. Serve immediately.

BAKED BRIE WITH CRANBERRY-APPLE CHUTNEY

Makes 6 servings

1   slice bacon, finely chopped
2   tablespoons chopped yellow
    onion
1   teaspoon minced shallot
½   Granny Smith apple, thinly
    sliced
3   tablespoons apple cider
    vinegar
2   tablespoons firmly packed
    light brown sugar
2   tablespoons sweetened dried
    cranberries
1   teaspoon chopped fresh
    thyme
¼   teaspoon kosher salt
⅛   teaspoon ground cinnamon
⅛   teaspoon ground ginger
1   (8-ounce) wheel Brie cheese
Toasted baguette slices, to serve
Garnish: fresh thyme, fresh
    parsley

1. Preheat oven to 350°. Line a rimmed baking sheet with foil.
2. In a medium skillet, cook bacon over medium heat until crisp. Remove bacon using a slotted spoon, and let drain on paper towels, reserving drippings in skillet.
3. Add onion and shallot to drippings in skillet. Cook, stirring frequently, until tender, about 5 minutes. Stir in apple, vinegar, brown sugar, cranberries, thyme, salt, cinnamon, and ginger; bring to a boil over medium heat. Reduce heat, and simmer, stirring frequently, until thickened, about 5 minutes. Remove from heat, and let cool slightly.
4. Place Brie on prepared pan. (Do not remove rind.) Bake until heated through, about 10 minutes. Place Brie on a serving plate; top with apple mixture and bacon. Serve with bread. Garnish with thyme and parsley, if desired.

KITCHEN TIP

If you're not a fan of Brie, the apple mixture is equally delicious spooned onto softened cream cheese.

BLT PIZZA

2	tablespoons unsalted butter
2	tablespoons all-purpose flour
1	cup whole milk
½	cup grated Parmesan cheese
1	clove garlic, minced
¼	teaspoon kosher salt
¼	teaspoon ground black pepper
4	slices thick-cut bacon
Pizza Dough (recipe follows)
1	cup cherry tomatoes
Garnish: baby romaine lettuce

1. Preheat oven to 450°.
2. In a small saucepan, melt butter over medium heat. Whisk in flour until smooth; cook, stirring constantly, until bubbly, about 1 minute. Gradually whisk in milk until smooth; cook until slightly thickened, about 2 minutes. Remove from heat; stir in cheese, garlic, salt, and pepper. Let cool to room temperature.
3. In a 9-inch square skillet, place bacon in an even layer.
4. Bake until slightly crisp, 10 to 15 minutes. Carefully remove bacon, and let drain on paper towels, reserving drippings in skillet.
5. On a lightly floured surface, divide Pizza Dough in half. Roll one portion of dough into an 11-inch square. (Reserve remaining dough for another use.) Carefully place dough in skillet. Fold edges under, and pinch to seal. Spread cheese sauce onto dough; top with bacon and tomatoes.
6. Bake until crust is golden brown, about 20 minutes. Let cool for 5 minutes. Garnish with lettuce, if desired.

PIZZA DOUGH
Makes 1 (14-inch) pizza crust

1⅓	cups warm water (105° to 110°)
1	(0.25-ounce) package active dry yeast
1	teaspoon sugar
3¼	cups all-purpose flour, divided
2	tablespoons plain yellow cornmeal
5	teaspoons extra-virgin olive oil, divided
2	teaspoons kosher salt

1. In a large bowl, stir together 1⅓ cups warm water, yeast, and sugar. Let stand until mixture is foamy, about 5 minutes. Add 2 cups flour, cornmeal, 3 teaspoons oil, and salt; beat with a mixer at medium speed for 2 minutes. Add 1 cup flour, stirring with a spoon until a soft, sticky dough forms and pulls away from sides of bowl.
2. Turn out dough onto a lightly floured surface, and knead until smooth and elastic, 5 to 6 minutes, using remaining ¼ cup flour as needed to keep dough from sticking to hands.
3. Lightly brush inside of a large bowl with remaining 2 teaspoons oil. Place dough in bowl, turning to grease top. Cover and let rise in a warm, draft-free place (75°) until doubled in size, about 1 hour and 15 minutes. Lightly punch down dough; turn out onto a lightly floured surface. Cover and let stand for 5 minutes.

KITCHEN TIP

You can also make this pizza
in a 10-inch round cast-iron
skillet. Roll dough to a 12-inch
circle, and proceed as directed.

CRUNCHY BACON RICE

2 cups basmati rice

2½ teaspoons kosher salt, divided

6 slices thick-cut bacon, chopped

1½ cups chopped yellow onion

½ teaspoon ground black pepper

3 cloves garlic, minced

2 tablespoons vegetable oil

½ cup toasted pecans, chopped

1. In a large saucepan, bring rice, 2 teaspoons salt, and water to cover by 2 inches to a boil over medium-high heat. Reduce heat; simmer until rice is almost tender, about 12 minutes. Drain.

2. In a 12-inch cast-iron skillet, cook bacon over medium heat until crisp, about 8 minutes. Remove bacon using a slotted spoon, and let drain on paper towels, reserving drippings in skillet.

3. Add onion, pepper, and remaining ½ teaspoon salt to drippings in skillet; cook until onions are softened. Stir in garlic; cook for 1 minute. Remove onion mixture from skillet with a slotted spoon.

4. Add 2 tablespoons oil to skillet. When oil is hot, spread half of rice into bottom of skillet, pressing gently. Sprinkle with half of onion mixture. Repeat with remaining rice and onion mixture. Cover surface of rice mixture with a sheet of parchment paper; cover with lid.

5. Cook over medium-low heat, without stirring, until rice is lightly browned on bottom, about 30 minutes. Using a spatula, turn rice, scraping browned bits from bottom of skillet into rice. Top with bacon and pecans. Serve immediately.

BACON-TOPPED FRENCH ONION SOUP

½ pound thick-cut bacon, chopped
1 cup unsalted butter
3 pounds yellow onions, sliced
4 cloves garlic, smashed
4 bay leaves
4 sprigs fresh thyme
2 teaspoons kosher salt
1 teaspoon ground black pepper
1 cup dry sherry
¼ cup all-purpose flour
2 (32-ounce) containers low-sodium beef broth
1 baguette, sliced ½ inch thick
4 cups shredded Gruyère cheese

1. In a large Dutch oven, cook bacon over medium heat until crisp. Remove bacon using a slotted spoon, and let drain on paper towels, reserving drippings in pot.

2. Melt butter with drippings in pot over medium heat. Add onion, garlic, bay leaves, thyme, salt, and pepper. Cook, stirring frequently, until onions are very soft and caramelized, about 35 minutes.

3. Stir in sherry; cook until liquid has evaporated, about 6 minutes. Discard bay leaves and thyme. Reduce heat to low; sprinkle flour onto onions. Cook, stirring constantly, for 5 minutes. Gradually stir in broth, and bring to a boil our medium heat. Reduce heat, and simmer for 15 minutes.

4. Preheat oven to 350°. Line a large baking sheet with foil. Place baguette slices on prepared pan. Bake until dry, about 10 minutes. Increase oven to broil.

5. Divide soup among broilerproof serving bowls. Top each with baguette slices and cheese. Place on baking sheet.

6. Broil until cheese is melted and bubbly, about 2 minutes. Top with bacon. Serve immediately.

LEEK AND BACON BREAKFAST CASSEROLE

Makes 6 servings

6 slices thick-cut bacon, chopped
3 cups chopped leeks
2 cloves garlic, minced
1 cup (1-inch) pieces asparagus
3 cups whole milk
¼ cup unsalted butter, melted
1 tablespoon chopped fresh thyme
1 teaspoon kosher salt
¼ teaspoon ground black pepper
6 large eggs
1 (12-ounce) loaf day-old French bread, cubed
1 cup shredded fontina cheese, divided
½ cup grated Parmesan cheese, divided

1. In a 10-inch cast-iron skillet, cook bacon over medium heat until crisp. Remove bacon using a slotted spoon, and let drain on paper towels, reserving drippings in skillet.
2. Add leeks and garlic to drippings in skillet; cook over medium-low heat for 3 minutes. Stir in asparagus; cover and cook, stirring occasionally, until asparagus is crisp-tender, about 8 minutes. Remove vegetables from skillet.
3. In a large bowl, whisk together milk, melted butter, thyme, salt, pepper, and eggs. Stir in bread, vegetables, ¾ cup fontina, and ¼ cup Parmesan. Cover and refrigerate for 4 hours.
4. Preheat oven to 350°.
5. Pour bread mixture into a 10-inch cast-iron skillet. Loosely cover with foil.
6. Bake for 25 minutes. Top with bacon, remaining ¼ cup fontina, and remaining ¼ cup Parmesan. Bake, uncovered, until puffed and golden, about 15 minutes more. Let stand for 10 minutes before serving.

KITCHEN TIP

If you don't have day-old bread, toast cubed fresh bread in the oven until dry and lightly browned.

BLACK BEAN AND BACON NACHOS

Makes 6 to 8 servings

¼ teaspoon ground cumin

¼ teaspoon chipotle chile powder

8 slices center-cut bacon

8 (6-inch) corn tortillas, cut into 6 wedges each

¼ teaspoon plus ⅛ teaspoon kosher salt, divided

1 cup shredded Monterey Jack cheese

½ cup shredded Cheddar cheese

½ cup canned black beans, rinsed and drained

1 jalapeño pepper, thinly sliced

½ cup cherry tomatoes, halved

¼ cup diced red onion

1 tablespoon chopped fresh cilantro

1 avocado, halved, pitted, peeled, and diced

1 tablespoon fresh lime juice

⅛ teaspoon garlic powder

Garnish: hot sauce

1. Preheat oven to 400°. Line a rimmed baking sheet with foil. Place a wire rack on baking sheet; spray rack with cooking spray.

2. In a small bowl, stir togther cumin and chile powder. Place bacon on prepared rack; sprinkle with spice mixture.

3. Bake until bacon is crisp, 15 to 20 minutes. Let cool slightly; chop.

4. On a large rimmed baking sheet, place tortilla wedges in an even layer. Spray with cooking spray; sprinkle with ¼ teaspoon salt.

5. Bake until crisp and lightly browned, 6 to 8 minutes. Top with cheeses, beans, and bacon. Bake until cheese is melted, 3 to 5 minutes more. Top with jalapeño, tomato, onion, and cilantro.

6. In a medium bowl, stir together avocado, lime juice, garlic powder, and remaining ⅛ teaspoon salt. Sprinkle onto nachos. Garnish with hot sauce, if desired.

BACON POTATO STACKS

2 pounds small russet potatoes, thinly sliced
8 slices bacon, cooked and crumbled
1 cup heavy whipping cream
2 cloves garlic, minced
1 teaspoon kosher salt
1 teaspoon chopped fresh thyme
½ teaspoon ground black pepper
⅛ teaspoon ground nutmeg
½ cup grated Pecorino cheese
Garnish: chopped fresh thyme

1. Preheat oven to 375°. Spray a 12-cup muffin pan with cooking spray. Place on a rimmed baking sheet.
2. Layer potatoes and bacon in prepared muffin cups until even with top of pan, beginning with potatoes and ending with bacon.
3. In a small saucepan, bring cream, garlic, salt, thyme, pepper, and nutmeg to a low boil over medium heat. Divide cream mixture among muffin cups, filling almost full. Sprinkle with cheese.
4. Bake until potatoes are fork-tender, 30 to 35 minutes. Let stand for 5 minutes. Run a knife around edges of cups to loosen. Using a fork, carefully remove potato stacks. Garnish with thyme, if desired.

KITCHEN TIP

It's best to leave the peel on potatoes for this recipe; the peel helps keep the slices from falling apart.

BACON-FRIED CHICKEN TENDERS

1½ cups whole buttermilk
1 tablespoon hot sauce
3 teaspoons kosher salt,
    plus more for sprinkling,
    divided
8 chicken tenderloins
8 slices bacon, chopped
3 cups vegetable oil
1 cup all-purpose flour
1 teaspoon ground black
    pepper, plus more for
    sprinkling
¾ teaspoon onion powder
Honey mustard and hot sauce,
    to serve

1. In a medium bowl, whisk together buttermilk, hot sauce, and 1½ teaspoons salt. Add chicken; cover and refrigerate for at least 6 hours or overnight.
2. In a 12-inch cast-iron skillet, cook bacon over medium-high heat, stirring occasionally, until crisp, about 10 minutes. Remove bacon using a slotted spoon, and let drain on paper towels, reserving drippings in skillet. Reserve ¼ cup bacon; finely chop remaining bacon.
3. Add oil to drippings in skillet, and heat over medium-high heat until a deep-fry thermometer registers 350°.
4. In a shallow dish, whisk together finely chopped bacon, flour, pepper, onion powder, and remaining 1½ teaspoons salt. Remove chicken from marinade, discarding marinade. Working in batches, dredge chicken in flour mixture, gently pressing to adhere and shaking off excess. Place chicken on a wire rack.
5. Fry chicken in batches, turning halfway through, until an instant-read thermometer inserted in thickest portion registers 165°, about 8 minutes. Let drain on paper towels. Sprinkle with salt, pepper, and reserved ¼ cup bacon. Serve with honey mustard and hot sauce.

flavored

WITH

BACON

Layered in a sandwich, stirred into
a side, or baked in a casserole,
bacon makes everything better

COLLARDS SALAD WITH WARM BACON VINAIGRETTE

½   cup apple cider vinegar
1   tablespoon sugar
2   teaspoons kosher salt, divided
1   large red onion, halved and
     thinly sliced
3   slices thick-cut bacon,
     chopped
1   tablespoon olive oil
2½   tablespoons sherry vinegar
1   tablespoon whole-grain
     mustard
1   teaspoon chopped fresh thyme
½   teaspoon ground black
     pepper
5   cups chopped stemmed
     collard greens
1   Fuji apple, thinly sliced
½   cup chopped pecans

1. In a small saucepan, bring cider vinegar, sugar, and 1½ teaspoons salt to a boil over medium-high heat. Remove from heat; stir in onion. Let stand at room temperature for 1 hour. Cover and refrigerate for up to 2 weeks.

2. In a medium skillet, cook bacon over medium heat until crisp, about 5 minutes. Remove from heat; add olive oil. Whisk in sherry vinegar, mustard, thyme, pepper, and remaining ½ teaspoon salt until combined.

3. In a large bowl, toss together collard greens, apple, pecans, ¾ cup pickled onions, and warm bacon mixture. Serve immediately. Reserve remaining onion for another use.

KITCHEN TIP

Kale, mustard greens, or turnip greens
can be used instead of collards.

BACON AND PIMIENTO CHEESE STUFFED JALAPEÑOS

Makes 12

1 cup shredded sharp Cheddar cheese

2 ounces cream cheese, softened

1 tablespoon mayonnaise

¾ teaspoon kosher salt, divided

¼ teaspoon ground black pepper

⅛ teaspoon garlic powder

1 (4-ounce) jar diced pimientos, drained

2 teaspoons canola oil

6 medium jalapeño peppers, halved lengthwise and seeded

4 slices bacon, cooked and crumbled

2 tablespoons chopped green onion

1. Preheat oven to 375°.

2. In a medium bowl, stir together Cheddar, cream cheese, mayonnaise, ½ teaspoon salt, black pepper, and garlic powder until combined; stir in pimientos until well combined.

3. In a 10-inch cast-iron skillet, heat oil over medium heat. Add jalapeños, cut side down. Cook until edges are lightly browned, about 2 minutes. Remove skillet from heat; remove jalapeños from skillet.

4. Sprinkle remaining ¼ teaspoon salt inside jalapeños. Spoon about 1 tablespoon cheese mixture into each jalapeño. Return jalapeños to skillet.

5. Bake until jalapeños are tender and cheese is melted, about 15 minutes. Top with bacon and green onion. Let stand for 5 minutes before serving.

KITCHEN TIP

Jalapeños can be prepared through step 4, covered, and refrigerated a day ahead; bake when you're ready to serve.

BACON-BRAISED BLACK-EYED PEAS

1   pound thick-cut bacon,
    chopped
1   large yellow onion,
    chopped
3   pounds shelled fresh or
    frozen black-eyed peas
6   cups low-sodium
    chicken broth
2   tablespoons firmly
    packed light brown
    sugar
2   teaspoons kosher salt
¼   teaspoon ground black
    pepper
2   dried red chile peppers
1   bay leaf

1. In a large Dutch oven, cook bacon over medium heat until crisp, about 10 minutes. Remove bacon using a slotted spoon, and let drain on paper towels, reserving ¼ cup drippings in pot.

2. Add onion to drippings in pot; cook, stirring occasionally, until tender, about 6 minutes. Stir in bacon, peas, broth, brown sugar, salt, black pepper, chiles, and bay leaf; bring to a boil over high heat. Reduce heat to medium-low; cook, partially covered, until peas are tender, about 30 minutes. Discard bay leaf and chiles before serving.

SMOKED CHEDDAR AND BACON CORN DIP

TORTILLAS

- 20 (6-inch) corn tortillas
- ½ cup canola oil
- 5 teaspoons kosher salt
- 5 teaspoons ground black pepper
- 5 teaspoons chili powder

DIP

- 4 ounces cream cheese, softened
- ¼ cup sour cream
- ¼ cup barbecue sauce
- 1 teaspoon Worcestershire sauce
- ½ teaspoon hot sauce
- ½ teaspoon ground red pepper
- 2 cups shredded smoked Cheddar cheese
- 1 cup fresh or thawed frozen corn kernels
- 4 slices bacon, cooked and crumbled

1. For tortillas: Place tortillas in a single layer on a large rimmed baking sheet. Brush oil onto both sides of tortillas; sprinkle with salt, pepper, and chili powder.

2. Spray a grill pan with cooking spray. Heat pan over medium heat.

3. Grill tortillas until grill marks form and tortillas are crisp, about 2 minutes per side; let cool. Break into pieces.

4. For dip: In a large bowl, stir together cream cheese, sour cream, barbecue sauce, Worcestershire, hot sauce, and red pepper until smooth. Stir in Cheddar, corn, and bacon until well combined. Serve with grilled tortillas.

BACON-ONION BURGERS

Makes 8

8 slices thick-cut bacon, chopped
½ cup chopped red onion
3 pounds ground round
1 teaspoon kosher salt
1 teaspoon ground black pepper
8 slices sharp Cheddar cheese
Hamburger buns, lettuce, ketchup, and sliced red onion, to serve

1. In a large cast-iron skillet, cook bacon over medium heat until crisp, about 10 minutes. Remove bacon using a slotted spoon, and let drain on paper towels, reserving drippings in skillet.
2. Add onion to drippings in skillet; cook until tender, 2 to 3 minutes. Remove from heat; let cool completely.
3. In a large bowl, gently stir together beef, bacon, onion, salt, and pepper. Divide mixture into 8 portions, and shape each portion into a 5-inch patty.
4. In same skillet, cook patties in batches over medium heat until desired degree of doneness is reached, 6 to 8 minutes per side. Add cheese during last minute of cooking. Serve on buns with lettuce, ketchup, and onion.

KITCHEN TIP

Be gentle when stirring together the beef mixture and shaping the patties; the more the meat is worked, the tougher your cooked burgers will be.

BACON AND SPINACH GRILLED CHEESE WITH FRIED EGG

Makes 4

8   slices multigrain bread
4   slices Gouda cheese
8   slices thick-cut bacon, cooked
4   tablespoons pickled jalapeño slices
2   cups fresh baby spinach
5   tablespoons salted butter, divided
4   large eggs
½   teaspoon ground black pepper

1. On half of bread slices, layer 1 slice Gouda, 2 slices bacon, 1 tablespoon jalapeño slices, ½ cup spinach, and remaining bread slices.

2. In a 12-inch cast-iron skillet, melt 2 tablespoons butter over medium heat. Add 2 sandwiches; cook until cheese is melted and bread is golden brown, 2 to 3 minutes per side. Remove sandwiches; keep warm. Repeat procedure with 2 tablespoons butter and remaining sandwiches. Wipe skillet clean.

3. In skillet, melt remaining 1 tablespoon butter over medium heat. Crack eggs into skillet; sprinkle with pepper. Cook until whites are set or to desired degree of doneness. Top each sandwich with an egg. Serve immediately.

BAKED TURNIP GREENS AND BACON DIP

6   slices bacon, chopped
1   cup chopped yellow onion
1   tablespoon minced fresh
     garlic
1   (16-ounce) package
     chopped turnip greens
2   cups low-sodium chicken
     broth
2   cups water
1   dried chile pepper
1   tablespoon kosher salt
1   tablespoon sugar
1½   (8-ounce) packages cream
     cheese, softened
½   cup sour cream
½   cup mayonnaise
¼   teaspoon ground red
     pepper
2   cups shredded fontina
     cheese
Toasted baguette slices, to serve
Garnish: shaved Parmesan
     cheese, crushed red pepper

1. In a medium Dutch oven, cook bacon over medium heat until crisp, about 8 minutes. Remove bacon using a slotted spoon, and let drain on paper towels, reserving drippings in pot.
2. Add onion and garlic to drippings in pot. Cook over medium-high heat, stirring occasionally, until tender, about 5 minutes. Stir in turnip greens in batches until wilted. Stir in broth, 2 cups water, chile, salt, and sugar; cook until greens are tender, about 20 minutes. Remove from heat, and let cool completely. Discard chile. Drain greens; thoroughly squeeze dry.
3. Preheat oven to 350°. Spray a 1½-quart baking dish with cooking spray.
4. In the work bowl of a food processor, pulse together greens, cream cheese, sour cream, mayonnaise, and red pepper until combined.
5. In a medium bowl, stir together greens mixture, fontina, and all but 2 tablespoons bacon. Spoon into prepared pan.
6. Bake until hot and bubbly, about 20 minutes. Top with remaining bacon; serve with bread. Garnish with Parmesan and red pepper, if desired.

SHRIMP AND GRITS CASSEROLE

GRITS

4	slices bacon, chopped
½	cup chopped red bell pepper
½	cup chopped yellow bell pepper
½	cup chopped yellow onion
2	cloves garlic, minced
2	cups chicken broth
2	cups whole milk
2	teaspoons kosher salt
½	teaspoon ground black pepper
1	cup quick-cooking yellow grits (not instant)
2	large eggs
1	cup shredded smoked Gouda cheese
1	cup shredded sharp Cheddar cheese

SHRIMP

1	tablespoon olive oil
½	teaspoon kosher salt
¼	teaspoon ground black pepper
1	pound large fresh shrimp, peeled and deveined (tails left on)
2	tablespoons chopped green onion

1. Preheat oven to 350°.
2. For grits: In a 10-inch cast-iron skillet, cook bacon over medium heat until crisp. Remove bacon using a slotted spoon, and let drain on paper towels, reserving drippings in skillet.
3. Add bell peppers and onion to drippings skillet; cook over medium heat, stirring occasionally, until softened. Add garlic; cook for 1 minute.
4. Stir in broth, milk, salt, and pepper; bring to a boil. Gradually whisk in grits until smooth. Reduce heat to low; cover and cook until grits are thickened and tender, about 6 minutes. Remove from heat.
5. In a medium bowl, beat eggs; slowly whisk ½ cup hot grits into eggs. Whisk egg mixture into grits in skillet. Stir in cheeses until melted.
6. Bake until grits are set, about 25 minutes.
7. Meanwhile, for shrimp: On a small rimmed baking sheet, drizzle oil. Place in oven until very hot, about 5 minutes. Sprinkle salt and pepper onto shrimp; place shrimp on hot baking sheet.
8. Bake until shrimp are pink and firm, about 9 minutes, turning once. Top grits with shrimp, green onion, and bacon. Serve immediately.

BACON AND SPINACH QUICHE

½ (14.1-ounce) package refrigerated piecrusts

12 slices bacon, chopped

1 (6-ounce) bag fresh baby spinach

1¼ cups shredded Swiss cheese

⅓ cup chopped green onion

3 large eggs

1⅓ cups heavy whipping cream

½ teaspoon ground black pepper

1. Preheat oven to 425°.

2. On a lightly floured surface, roll piecrust into an 11-inch circle. Transfer to a 9-inch pie plate, pressing into bottom and up sides. Fold edges under, and crimp as desired. Prick bottom and sides of crust with a fork.

3. Bake for 5 minutes. Let cool completely. Reduce oven temperature to 350°.

4. Meanwhile, in a large skillet, cook bacon over medium-high heat until crisp. Remove bacon using a slotted spoon, and let drain on paper towels, reserving 1 tablespoon drippings in skillet.

5. Add spinach to drippings in skillet; cook, stirring frequently, until just wilted, about 3 minutes. Let spinach drain on paper towels.

6. Layer cheese, bacon, green onion, and spinach in prepared crust. In a medium bowl, whisk together eggs, cream, and pepper; pour onto cheese mixture in crust.

7. Bake until center is just set, 40 to 45 minutes, covering edges of crust with foil to prevent excess browning, if needed. Let stand for 10 minutes before serving.

BACON AND CHIVE EGG SALAD

8   hard-cooked large eggs, chopped
½   cup cooked chopped bacon
¼   cup mayonnaise
1   tablespoon chopped fresh chives
2   teaspoons Dijon mustard
2   teaspoons sweet pickle relish
½   teaspoon kosher salt
½   teaspoon garlic powder
¼   teaspoon ground black pepper
Garnish: chopped fresh chives

1. In a medium bowl, stir together eggs, three-fourths of bacon, mayonnaise, chives, mustard, relish, salt, garlic powder, and pepper until combined. Top with remaining bacon, and garnish with chives, if desired. Cover and refrigerate for up to 3 days.

KITCHEN TIP

Add a chopped stalk of celery for more texture and crunch.

ULTIMATE SOUTHERN MAC AND CHEESE

½   cup unsalted butter
½   cup all-purpose flour
⅔   cup minced yellow onion
4   cups whole milk
4½ cups shredded sharp white Cheddar cheese, divided
2½ cups shredded smoked Gouda cheese, divided
1   pound thick-cut bacon, chopped and cooked
3   tablespoons whole-grain mustard
2   tablespoons chopped fresh parsley
1½ teaspoons kosher salt
½   teaspoon ground black pepper
½   teaspoon ground red pepper
¼   teaspoon ground nutmeg
1   (16-ounce) package elbow macaroni, cooked according to package directions

1. Preheat oven to 350°.
2. In a 12-inch cast-iron skillet, melt butter over medium-high heat. Whisk in flour; cook, whisking constantly, until lightly browned, about 15 minutes. Add onion; cook, stirring frequently, until tender, 3 to 4 minutes. Gradually whisk in milk until smooth; cook, whisking frequently, until mixture begins to thicken, about 8 minutes.
3. Whisk 4 cups Cheddar, 1¾ cups Gouda, bacon, mustard, parsley, salt, peppers, and nutmeg into sauce until cheese is melted. Stir in cooked pasta; top with remaining ½ cup Cheddar and remaining ¾ cup Gouda.
4. Bake until top is golden brown, 20 to 25 minutes. Let stand for 15 minutes before serving.

KITCHEN TIP
Use any short, tubular pasta you prefer in this dish.

BACON AND SAUSAGE DEEP-DISH PIZZA

Makes 1 (12-inch) pizza

4   slices thick-cut bacon, chopped
½   pound ground hot Italian sausage
1   cup chopped smoked sausage
1   cup chopped yellow onion
1   cup chopped red bell pepper
1   cup chopped yellow bell pepper
2   cloves garlic, minced
1½   cups crushed tomatoes
2   tablespoons chopped fresh parsley
1   tablespoon chopped fresh oregano
1   teaspoon fennel seeds, crushed
½   teaspoon kosher salt
Pizza Dough (recipe on page 50)
2   cups shredded provolone cheese, divided
1   cup shredded sharp Cheddar cheese
¼   cup pepperoni slices

1. Preheat oven to 450°.

2. In a 12-inch cast-iron skillet, cook bacon over medium heat until crisp, 6 to 8 minutes. Remove bacon using a slotted spoon, and let drain on paper towels. Reserve 1 tablespoon drippings in a small bowl.

3. To skillet, add sausages, onion, and bell peppers; cook, stirring occasionally, until ground sausage is browned and crumbly, 8 to 10 minutes; drain.

4. Stir in garlic; cook for 1 minute. Stir in tomatoes, parsley, oregano, fennel seeds, and salt; cook, stirring occasionally, for 10 minutes. Remove sausage mixture from skillet. Wipe skillet clean.

5. Brush reserved 1 tablespoon drippings into skillet. Place skillet in oven until very hot, 5 to 6 minutes.

6. On a lightly floured surface, roll Pizza Dough into a 14-inch circle. Carefully transfer dough to hot skillet, letting excess dough extend over sides of pan. Sprinkle 1 cup provolone into dough; spread sausage mixture onto cheese. Fold edges of dough over filling (dough will not completely cover filling). Sprinkle Cheddar, pepperoni, and remaining 1 cup provolone onto filling.

7. Bake until crust is golden brown and cheese is melted, 15 to 20 minutes. Top with bacon. Let stand for 15 minutes before serving.

BACON AND TATER TOT BREAKFAST CASSEROLE

Makes 10 to 12 servings

1 tablespoon bacon drippings
3 large jalapeño peppers, seeded and chopped
1 small yellow onion, diced
2 cloves garlic, minced
2 pounds thick-cut bacon, cooked and crumbled
1 (32-ounce) package frozen Tater Tots
2 cups shredded sharp Cheddar cheese
½ cup chopped fresh parsley
8 large eggs
1½ cups whole milk
½ cup sour cream
2 teaspoons kosher salt
½ teaspoon ground black pepper
Garnish: chopped fresh parsley, hot sauce

1. Preheat oven to 350°.
2. In a large skillet, heat bacon drippings over medium-high heat. Add jalapeño and onion; cook, stirring occasionally, until tender, about 5 minutes. Add garlic; cook until fragrant, about 1 minute. Remove from heat.
3. In a large bowl, stir together bacon, Tater Tots, cheese, parsley, and jalapeño mixture until combined. Spoon into a 13x9-inch baking dish.
4. In same large bowl, whisk together eggs, milk, sour cream, salt, and pepper until smooth; pour onto Tater Tot mixture.
5. Bake until center is set, 45 to 50 minutes. Let stand for 10 minutes before serving. Garnish with parsley and hot sauce, if desired.

KITCHEN TIP

This casserole can be assembled through step 3, covered, and refrigerated overnight. Uncover and let it stand at room temperature for 30 mintues before baking as directed.

BACON AND CANE SYRUP BAKED BEANS

1   **pound thick-cut bacon, chopped**
1   **small yellow onion, chopped**
2   **cloves garlic, minced**
4   **(15-ounce) cans navy beans, rinsed and drained**
½   **cup cane syrup**
½   **cup apple cider vinegar**
3   **tablespoons ketchup**
2   **tablespoons Dijon mustard**
1½ **tablespoons light brown sugar**
2   **teaspoons kosher salt**
2   **teaspoons chili powder**
1   **teaspoon ground black pepper**

1. Preheat oven to 400°.

2. In a 12-inch ovenproof skillet, cook bacon over medium heat, stirring occasionally, until crisp, about 12 minutes. Remove bacon using a slotted spoon, and let drain on paper towels, reserving drippings in skillet.

3. Add onion to drippings in skillet; cook, stirring frequently, until tender, about 8 minutes. Stir in garlic; cook for 1 minute. Stir in beans, syrup, vinegar, ketchup, mustard, brown sugar, salt, chili powder, and pepper; bring to a boil. Stir in half of bacon.

4. Bake, uncovered, until liquid thickens, about 45 minutes. Stir in remaining bacon; let stand for 5 minutes before serving.

KITCHEN TIP

Maple syrup or sorghum syrup can be used in place of cane syrup.

CHICKEN BACON RANCH CASSEROLE

8   slices thick-cut bacon, chopped
2   pounds boneless skinless chicken breasts, cut into ¾-inch pieces
1   (1-ounce) package ranch seasoning mix
3   cloves garlic, minced
2   cups heavy whipping cream
½   cup grated Parmesan cheese
2   cups large elbow macaroni, cooked according to package directions
½   cup chopped fresh parsley
1   cup shredded mozzarella cheese
½   cup shredded sharp Cheddar cheese

1. Preheat oven to 375°.
2. In a 10-inch cast-iron skillet, cook bacon over medium heat until crisp. Remove bacon using a slotted spoon, and let drain on paper towels, reserving 1 tablespoon drippings in skillet and remaining drippings in a small bowl.
3. In a large bowl, stir together chicken and ranch seasoning. Add chicken to drippings in skillet; cook until browned on all sides, about 6 minutes. Remove from skillet; wipe skillet clean.
4. Heat 2 tablespoons reserved drippings in skillet over medium heat. Add garlic; cook for 30 seconds. Gradually whisk in cream; bring to a low boil. Cook until slightly thickened, about 3 minutes. Whisk in Parmesan until melted. Remove from heat.
5. Stir chicken, half of cooked bacon, cooked pasta, and parsley into sauce. Sprinkle mozzarella, Cheddar, and remaining bacon onto mixture.
6. Bake until golden brown and bubbly, about 25 minutes. Let stand for 10 minutes before serving.

BRAISED CHICKEN WITH MUSHROOMS AND BACON

1 tablespoon unsalted butter
1 tablespoon canola oil
1 teaspoon kosher salt
½ teaspoon ground black pepper
4 bone-in skin-on chicken legs
4 bone-in skin-on chicken thighs
½ pound thick-cut bacon, chopped
4 cups chopped carrots
2 (4-ounce) packages gourmet blend mushrooms
3 cloves garlic, minced
2 cups dry red wine, such as Cabernet Sauvignon
2 cups chicken broth
2 tablespoons cornstarch
1 tablespoon water
Mashed potatoes, to serve

1. Preheat oven to 300°.
2. In a large Dutch oven, melt butter with oil over medium-high heat. Sprinkle salt and pepper all over chicken. Cook chicken until browned, 2 to 3 minutes per side. Remove from pot.
3. Add bacon to pot. Cook, stirring frequently, until crisp, about 10 minutes. Add carrots; cook, stirring frequently, until softened, about 4 minutes. Stir in mushrooms and garlic; cook, stirring frequently, until tender, about 5 minutes. Stir in wine; bring to a low boil. Cook for 10 minutes, stirring occasionally. Stir in broth, and return chicken to pot. Bring to a boil; cover pot.
4. Bake until chicken is very tender, about 1 hour and 30 minutes. Remove chicken from pot.
5. In a small bowl, whisk together cornstarch and 1 tablespoon water until smooth; stir cornstarch mixture into cooking liquid in pot. Bring to a boil over medium heat; cook, stirring occasionally, until thickened, about 15 minutes. Return chicken to pot; cook until heated through. Serve with mashed potatoes.

FRIED GREEN TOMATO AND PIMIENTO CHEESE BLTS

Makes 4 to 6

PIMIENTO CHEESE
1 (8-ounce) package cream cheese, softened
½ cup mayonnaise
1 (12-ounce) jar roasted red peppers, drained and roughly chopped
1 (4-ounce) jar diced pimientos, drained
2 (8-ounce) packages extra-sharp Cheddar cheese, shredded
1 teaspoon hot sauce
1 teaspoon Worcestershire sauce
1 teaspoon sugar
1 teaspoon kosher salt
1 teaspoon ground black pepper
½ teaspoon ground red pepper

FRIED GREEN TOMATOES
Vegetable oil, for frying
1½ cups whole buttermilk
1 cup plain yellow cornmeal
1 cup all-purpose flour
1½ teaspoons kosher salt
1 teaspoon ground black pepper
½ teaspoon ground red pepper
4 green tomatoes, sliced ¼ inch thick

Toasted sandwich bread, lettuce, cooked bacon, and sliced red tomatoes, to serve

1. For pimiento cheese: In the work bowl of a food processor, pulse together cream cheese and mayonnaise until smooth. Add peppers and pimientos; pulse until coarsely chopped.
2. Add Cheddar, hot sauce, Worcestershire, sugar, salt, black pepper, and red pepper; pulse until mixture is almost smooth. Cover and refrigerate for up to 5 days.
3. For fried green tomatoes: In a large Dutch oven, pour oil to a depth of 4 inches, and heat over medium heat until a deep-fry thermometer registers 350°.
4. Place buttermilk in a shallow dish. In another shallow dish, whisk together cornmeal, flour, salt, and peppers. Working in batches, dip tomatoes in buttermilk, letting excess drip off. Dredge tomatoes in cornmeal mixture, gently shaking off excess.
5. Fry tomatoes in batches until golden brown, 5 to 6 minutes. Remove from oil, and let drain on paper towels.
6. Spread pimiento cheese onto bread slices; top with lettuce, bacon, fried green tomatoes, and red tomatoes as desired.

BACON CHEESEBURGER PULL-APART SLIDERS

Makes 12

1 (12-ounce) package Hawaiian sweet rolls, halved lengthwise
2 cups shredded sharp Cheddar cheese, divided
1 tablespoon olive oil
1 pound ground sirloin
½ cup minced yellow onion
1 tablespoon Montreal steak seasoning
3½ teaspoons Worcestershire sauce, divided
1 tablespoon tomato paste
¼ cup chopped green onion
½ pound bacon, chopped and cooked
2 tablespoons melted bacon drippings
1 tablespoon firmly packed light brown sugar
1 tablespoon Dijon mustard
1 teaspoon sesame seeds

1. Preheat oven to 350°. Place bottom of rolls, cut side up, in a 9-inch square cast-iron skillet. Top with 1 cup cheese.

2. In a large cast-iron skillet, heat oil over medium-high. Add beef, onion, and steak seasoning; cook, stirring occasionally, until beef is browned and crumbly and onion is tender, about 8 minutes. Stir in 1½ teaspoons Worcestershire and tomato paste; cook for 1 minute. Stir in green onion. Spoon beef mixture in an even layer onto rolls; top with bacon, remaining 1 cup cheese, and top of rolls, cut side down.

3. In a small bowl, whisk together melted bacon drippings, brown sugar, mustard, and remaining 2 teaspoons Worcestershire until smooth. Brush onto rolls; sprinkle with sesame seeds.

4. Bake until golden brown and heated through, about 20 minutes. Serve immediately.

SAVORY GREEN TOMATO COBBLER

2 pounds green tomatoes, cut into 1-inch pieces (about 6½ cups)
½ cup chopped fresh basil
2 tablespoons cornstarch
2 teaspoons kosher salt, divided
1 teaspoon ground black pepper, divided
¾ pound thick-cut bacon, chopped
1½ cups all-purpose flour
2¼ teaspoons baking powder
1½ tablespoons sugar
½ cup shredded extra-sharp Cheddar cheese
½ cup plus 1 tablespoon whole buttermilk, divided
⅓ cup unsalted butter, melted

1. Preheat oven to 350°.
2. In a large bowl, stir together tomatoes, basil, cornstarch, 1 teaspoon salt, and ¾ teaspoon pepper.
3. In a 10-inch ovenproof skillet, cook bacon over medium-high heat until browned and crisp, about 10 minutes. Remove bacon from skillet using a slotted spoon, and let drain on paper towels, reserving 2 tablespoons drippings in skillet.
4. Add tomato mixture to skillet; cook over medium-low heat, stirring frequently, until tomatoes begin to soften, 5 to 7 minutes. Remove from heat.
5. Meanwhile, in another large bowl, whisk together flour, baking powder, sugar, and remaining 1 teaspoon salt; stir in cheese. Stir in ½ cup buttermilk and melted butter just until combined. Drop dough by scant ¼ cupfuls onto tomato mixture. Brush remaining 1 tablespoon buttermilk onto biscuits; sprinkle with remaining ¼ teaspoon pepper.
6. Bake until biscuits are golden brown and filling is bubbly, 25 to 30 minutes. Let stand for 10 minutes before serving.

baked

WITH

BACON

Packed with flavor, bacon is
the perfect addition to sweet
and savory baked goods

BACON UPSIDE-DOWN CORNBREAD

5   slices thick-cut bacon
6   slices thick-cut bacon, chopped
Melted bacon drippings or vegetable oil, as needed
2   cups plain white cornmeal
1   cup all-purpose flour
1   tablespoon baking powder
1   tablespoon chopped fresh thyme
1½ teaspoons kosher salt
½   teaspoon ground black pepper
2½ cups whole buttermilk
2   large eggs
1½ cups shredded Gruyère cheese
Garnish: chopped fresh thyme

1. In a 10-inch cast-iron skillet, cook bacon slices over medium-high heat, turning frequently until almost crisp, about 10 minutes. Remove bacon, and let drain on paper towels. Pour off drippings into a small bowl; reserve.
2. Add chopped bacon to skillet; cook over medium-high heat, stirring occasionally, until crisp, about 12 minutes. Remove chopped bacon using a slotted spoon, and let drain on paper towels. Add drippings from skillet to bowl of reserved drippings; add additional melted bacon drippings or oil as needed to equal 8 tablespoons. Wipe skillet clean.
3. Preheat oven to 425°.
4. Add 2 tablespoons reserved bacon drippings to skillet; place skillet in oven while oven preheats.
5. In a large bowl, whisk together cornmeal, flour, baking powder, thyme, salt, and pepper. In a medium bowl, whisk together buttermilk, eggs, and remaining 6 tablespoons reserved bacon drippings. Stir buttermilk mixture into cornmeal mixture just until dry ingredients are moistened; stir in cheese and reserved chopped bacon until combined. Carefully place reserved 5 slices bacon in bottom of preheated skillet. Gently spread batter onto bacon slices.
6. Bake until golden brown and a wooden pick inserted in center comes out clean, about 30 minutes. Let cool in pan on a wire rack for 10 minutes. Invert onto a serving plate. Garnish with thyme, if desired.

KITCHEN TIP

Wiping the skillet clean removes any caramelized bits from the pan so the cornbread crust doesn't bake too dark; skip that step if you prefer a darker crust.

BACON LATTICE APPLE PIE

Makes 1 (9-inch) pie

6 slices thick-cut applewood-smoked bacon

½ (14.1-ounce) package refrigerated piecrusts

6 cups (¼-inch-thick) sliced unpeeled Gala apples (about 4 large)

⅓ cup granulated sugar

3 tablespoons all-purpose flour

1 tablespoon fresh lemon juice

1¾ teaspoons apple pie spice, divided

¼ cup firmly packed dark brown sugar

1. Preheat oven to 375°.

2. Spray a wire rack with cooking spray; place rack on a large rimmed baking sheet. Place bacon on prepared rack.

3. Bake for 10 minutes. Remove from oven; let cool.

4. On a lightly floured surface, roll dough into an 11-inch circle. Transfer to a 9-inch pie plate, pressing into bottom and up sides. Fold edges under, and crimp as desired.

5. In a large bowl, stir together apples, granulated sugar, flour, lemon juice, and 1½ teaspoons pie spice. Spoon into prepared crust.

6. Bake for 30 minutes. Carefully arrange bacon slices in a lattice pattern on apple mixture, trimming ends of bacon as needed. Sprinkle remaining ¼ teaspoon pie spice and brown sugar onto bacon.

7. Bake until crust is golden brown and filling is bubbly, about 20 minutes more, covering with foil during last 10 minutes of baking to prevent excess browning, if necessary. Let cool completely on a wire rack before slicing.

KITCHEN TIP

Braeburn, Honeycrisp, or Pink Lady apples can be substituted for Gala apples in this pie.

BACON-CHEDDAR BISCUITS

Makes 10 to 12

2½ cups self-rising flour
1   tablespoon sugar
1¼ teaspoons ground black
    pepper, divided
½   cup cold bacon
    drippings
2   tablespoons cold
    unsalted butter, cubed
1   cup shredded sharp
    Cheddar cheese
½   cup crumbled cooked
    bacon
¾   cup cold whole
    buttermilk
1   large egg
1   tablespoon water

1. Preheat oven to 425°. Line a large baking sheet with parchment paper.
2. In a large bowl, whisk together flour, sugar, and 1 teaspoon pepper. Using a pastry blender, cut in bacon drippings and cold butter until mixture is crumbly; stir in cheese and cooked bacon. Stir in buttermilk just until combined.
3. Turn out dough onto a heavily floured surface. Fold dough in half until it comes together, 3 to 4 times. Pat or roll dough to 1-inch thickness. Using a knife dipped in flour, cut dough into 2-inch squares. Place biscuits 2 inches apart on prepared pan.
4. In a small bowl, whisk together egg and 1 tablespoon water; lightly brush onto biscuits. Sprinkle remaining ¼ teaspoon pepper onto biscuits. Freeze until cold, about 10 minutes.
5. Bake until golden brown, 12 to 14 minutes. Let cool on pan for 5 minutes; serve warm.

⊦ KITCHEN TIP ⊦

Tuck a fried egg in one of these biscuits
for a scrumptious breakfast sandwich.

CHOCOLATE CHIP COOKIES WITH BACON

Makes about 36

½   cup unsalted butter,
     softened
½   cup cold bacon drippings
¾   cup granulated sugar
¾   cup firmly packed light
     brown sugar
2   large eggs
1   teaspoon vanilla extract
2¼   cups all-purpose flour
1   teaspoon baking soda
1   teaspoon kosher salt
3   cups bittersweet
     chocolate chips
1   (12-ounce) package
     center-cut bacon,
     cooked and crumbled
Garnish: flaked sea salt

1. Preheat oven to 375°.
2. In a large bowl, beat butter, cold drippings, and sugars, with a mixer at medium speed until fluffy, 3 to 4 minutes, stopping to scrape sides of bowl. Add eggs, one at a time, beating well after each addition. Beat in vanilla.
3. In a medium bowl, whisk together flour, baking soda, and salt. With mixer on low speed, gradually add flour mixture to butter mixture, beating just until combined. Stir in chocolate chips and bacon. Using a 1½-inch spring-loaded scoop, drop dough 2 inches apart on a 15-inch cast-iron baking sheet or a large parchment paper-lined baking sheet.
4. Bake until edges are golden brown, 9 to 11 minutes. Let cool on pan for 2 minutes. Remove from pan, and let cool completely on wire racks. Garnish with sea salt, if desired. Store in an airtight container for up to 2 days.

KITCHEN TIP

If you use a cast-iron baking sheet, let it
cool between baking each batch of cookies.

SWEET POTATO MUFFINS WITH BACON

Makes 10 to 12

MUFFINS

1	cup self-rising flour
¾	cup sugar
1	teaspoon pumpkin pie spice
1	cup mashed cooked sweet potato*
1	large egg
5	tablespoons unsalted butter, melted
2	tablespoons melted bacon drippings
1	teaspoon vanilla extract
½	teaspoon orange zest
½	cup crumbled cooked bacon

GLAZE

1	cup confectioners' sugar
2	tablespoons whole milk
½	teaspoon orange zest
⅛	teaspoon kosher salt

1. Preheat oven to 375°. Line 10 to 12 muffin cups with paper liners.

2. For muffins: In a large bowl, whisk together flour, sugar, and pie spice. In a medium bowl, whisk together sweet potato, egg, melted butter, melted drippings, vanilla, and zest. Stir sweet potato mixture into flour mixture just until combined. Spoon batter into prepared muffin cups, filling two-thirds full. Sprinkle with bacon.

3. Bake until a wooden pick inserted in center comes out clean, about 17 minutes. Let cool in pans for 5 minutes. Remove from pan, and let cool completely on a wire rack.

4. For glaze: In a medium bowl, whisk together all ingredients until smooth. Drizzle onto muffins. Store in an airtight container for up to 2 days.

We used Bruce's Cut Sweet Potatoes in Syrup, drained before mashing.

BACON-PEANUT BUTTER SANDWICH COOKIES

Makes about 15

COOKIES

¾   cup creamy peanut butter
½   cup unsalted butter, softened
1   cup firmly packed light brown sugar
1   large egg
1   teaspoon vanilla extract
1½ cups all-purpose flour
1   teaspoon baking soda
½   teaspoon kosher salt

FILLING

½   cup creamy peanut butter
1   tablespoon unsalted butter, softened
3   cups confectioners' sugar
¼   cup whole milk
½   cup finely crumbled cooked bacon

Garnish: finely crumbled cooked bacon

1. Preheat oven to 350°. Line baking sheets with parchment paper.
2. For cookies: In a large bowl, beat peanut butter, butter, and brown sugar with a mixer at medium speed until creamy, 3 to 4 minutes, stopping to scrape sides of bowl. Add egg, beating well. Beat in vanilla.
3. In a medium bowl, whisk together flour, baking soda, and salt. With mixer on low speed, gradually add flour mixture to butter mixture, beating until combined. Roll dough into 1-inch balls; place 2 inches apart on prepared pans. Using a fork dipped in flour, press a crosshatch pattern into cookies.
4. Bake until lightly browned, 10 to 12 minutes. Let cool on pans for 3 minutes. Remove from pans, and let cool completely on wire racks.
5. For filling: In a medium bowl, beat peanut butter and butter with a mixer at medium speed until creamy. Gradually add confectioners' sugar and milk, beating until smooth; beat in bacon.
6. Spread filling onto flat side of half of cookies. Top with remaining cookies, flat side down. Roll sides of cookies in crumbled bacon, if desired. Store in an airtight container for up to 2 days.

MAPLE-BACON MONKEY BREAD

1½ cups sugar, divided
2 teaspoons ground
 cinnamon
2 (16.3-ounce) cans
 refrigerated biscuits,
 each quartered and
 rolled into balls
½ cup unsalted butter
½ cup maple syrup
1 (16-ounce) package
 maple bacon, cooked
 and crumbled
1 cup chopped pecans

1. Preheat oven to 350°. Spray a 15-cup Bundt pan with cooking spray.
2. In a large bowl, whisk together ¾ cup sugar and cinnamon. Working in batches, roll biscuit pieces in cinnamon sugar to coat; shake off excess. Reserve remaining cinnamon sugar.
3. In a small saucepan, bring butter, maple syrup, and remaining ¾ cup sugar to a boil over medium-high heat, stirring until sugar dissolves. Stir in reserved cinnamon sugar; cook until melted, 2 to 3 minutes.
4. Sprinkle ¼ cup bacon and ¼ cup pecans in bottom of prepared pan. Drizzle one-fourth of sugar mixture onto nuts. Add one layer of biscuit pieces to pan; repeat layers three times.
5. Bake until biscuits are cooked through, about 35 minutes. Let cool in pan for 10 minutes; invert onto a serving platter. Serve immediately.

KITCHEN TIP

No maple syrup? Use an equal amount of honey, cane syrup, or dark corn syrup.

CHEESY BACON BISCUIT BITES

Makes 32

2 (16.3-ounce) cans refrigerated homestyle biscuits*, each biscuit halved crosswise
1 (8-ounce) package shredded Colby-Jack cheese
1 (12-ounce) package thick-cut bacon, cooked and crumbled
1 large egg, beaten
Everything bagel seasoning

1. Preheat oven to 350°. Spray a 12-inch cast-iron skillet with baking spray with flour.
2. Gently press each biscuit piece to ¼-inch thickness. Spoon about 1 tablespoon cheese and 1 teaspoon bacon into center of each biscuit piece; wrap biscuit dough around filling, pinching seams to seal. Starting around sides of pan, place biscuits in skillet, seam side down, in concentric circles. (Biscuits will fit snuggly with sides touching.) Brush egg onto biscuits; sprinkle with everything bagel seasoning.
3. Bake until golden brown, 28 to 30 minutes. Let cool on a wire rack for 10 minutes before serving.

*We used Pillsbury Grands! Southern Homestyle Buttermilk Biscuits.

KITCHEN TIP

For a kick of heat, use Monterey Jack cheese with peppers instead of Colby-Jack or add a sprinkle of crushed red pepper on top.

MAPLE, BACON, AND BOURBON CUPCAKES

Makes 24

CUPCAKES

1   cup unsalted butter,
     softened
1¼   cups granulated sugar
3   large eggs
⅓   cup whole milk
⅓   cup bourbon
2   teaspoons vanilla extract
2⅓   cups self-rising flour

GLAZE

1½   cups confectioners' sugar,
     sifted
4   tablespoons maple syrup
1   teaspoon fresh lemon juice

3   slices bacon, cooked and
     crumbled

1. Preheat oven to 350°. Line 24 muffin cups with paper liners.

2. For cupcakes: In a large bowl, beat butter and granulated sugar with a mixer at medium speed until fluffy, 3 to 4 minutes, stopping to scrape sides of bowl. Add eggs, one at a time, beating well after each addition.

3. In a small bowl, whisk together milk, bourbon, and vanilla. With mixer on low speed, gradually add flour to butter mixture alternately with milk mixture, beginning and ending with flour, beating just until combined after each addition. Divide batter among prepared muffin cups.

4. Bake until a wooden pick inserted in center comes out clean, 18 to 20 minutes. Let cool in pans for 5 minutes. Remove from pans, and let cool completely on wire racks.

5. For glaze: In a medium bowl, whisk together confectioners' sugar, 4 tablespoons maple syrup, and lemon juice until smooth. Drizzle onto muffins; top with bacon. Store in an airtight container for up to 2 days.

BACON-PECAN STICKY ROLLS

Makes 8

TOPPING

⅓ cup unsalted butter
2 tablespoons granulated sugar
2 tablespoons firmly packed dark brown sugar
3 tablespoons honey
¼ teaspoon ground cinnamon
½ cup chopped toasted pecans
⅓ cup cooked crumbled bacon

ROLLS

1 (8-ounce) can refrigerated crescent dough sheet
1 tablespoon unsalted butter, melted
⅓ cup cooked crumbled bacon
2 tablespoons firmly packed dark brown sugar
¼ teaspoon ground cinnamon

1. Preheat oven to 375°. Spray an 8-inch round cake pan with baking spray with flour.
2. For topping: In a small saucepan, cook butter, sugars, honey, and cinnamon over medium heat, stirring occasionally, until butter is melted, about 4 minutes. Pour butter mixture into prepared pan; sprinkle with pecans and bacon.
3. For rolls: On a lightly floured surface, unroll dough. Brush melted butter onto dough; sprinkle with bacon, brown sugar, and cinnamon. Starting at one short side, tightly roll up dough into a log; pinch seam to seal. Using a serrated knife, cut log crosswise into 8 slices. Place slices, cut side up, about 1 inch apart on pecan mixture in pan.
4. Bake until golden brown, about 18 minutes. Let cool on a wire rack for 10 minutes. Carefully invert rolls onto a serving plate. Serve warm.

FUDGY BACON BROWNIES WITH CARAMEL AND SEA SALT

BROWNIES

1   cup unsalted butter, softened
2¼   cups sugar
4   large eggs
1½   cups all-purpose flour
1   cup unsweetened cocoa powder
½   teaspoon baking powder
½   teaspoon kosher salt
2   tablespoons whole milk
2   teaspoons vanilla extract
½   cup chopped semisweet chocolate
⅓   cup crumbled cooked bacon

FROSTING

½   cup heavy whipping cream
1   teaspoon unsalted butter
1   (4-ounce) bar semisweet chocolate, chopped

CARAMEL

1   cup sugar
¼   cup water
1   tablespoon light corn syrup
1   tablespoon cold unsalted butter
½   cup warm heavy whipping cream
½   teaspoon vanilla extract
¼   teaspoon kosher salt

⅔   cup crumbled cooked bacon
1   tablespoon flaked sea salt

1. Preheat oven to 325°. Line a 13x9-inch baking pan with foil, letting excess extend over sides of pan; spray foil with baking spray with flour.

2. For brownies: In a large bowl, beat butter and sugar with a mixer at medium speed until fluffy, 3 to 4 minutes, stopping to scrape sides of bowl. Add eggs, one at a time, beating well after each addition.

3. In a medium bowl, sift together flour, cocoa, baking powder, and salt. With mixer on low speed, gradually add flour mixture to butter mixture, beating until combined. Beat in milk and vanilla. Stir in semisweet chocolate and bacon. (Batter will be thick.) Spread batter into prepared pan.

4. Bake until a wooden pick inserted in center comes out clean, about 27 minutes. Let cool completely on a wire rack.

5. For frosting: In a medium microwave-safe bowl, heat cream and butter on high until hot but not boiling, about 30 seconds. Add semisweet chocolate; let stand for 1 minute. Stir until chocolate is melted. Spread onto brownies. Let stand until frosting is set, about 3 hours.

6. For caramel: In a large heavy-bottomed saucepan, sprinkle sugar. In a small bowl, stir together ¼ cup water and corn syrup. Pour all over sugar, swirling to coat. Cook over medium-high heat, without stirring, until mixture begins to turn golden brown, about 5 minutes. Remove from heat; stir in cold butter until melted. (Mixture will foam.) Stir in warm cream until smooth; stir in vanilla and salt. Let cool completely.

7. Using excess foil as handles, remove from pan; cut into bars. Drizzle caramel onto brownies; sprinkle with bacon and salt. Store in an airtight container for up to 2 days. Refrigerate remaining caramel in an airtight container for up to 2 weeks.

BACON-PEANUT BANANA BREAD

Makes 1 (8x4-inch) loaf

TOPPING

2   slices bacon, finely chopped
¼   cup all-purpose flour
3   tablespoons firmly packed
     light brown sugar
¼   teaspoon ground cinnamon
1   tablespoon unsalted
     butter, melted
2   tablespoons chopped
     salted peanuts

BREAD

6   slices bacon, chopped
1⅔ cups all-purpose flour
1   teaspoon baking powder
½   teaspoon kosher salt
1½ cups mashed ripe banana
      (about 3 medium)
1   cup firmly packed light
      brown sugar
½   cup unsalted butter, melted
¼   cup whole buttermilk
2   large eggs
1   teaspoon vanilla extract
¾   teaspoon ground cinnamon
¼   cup chopped salted peanuts

GLAZE

½   cup confectioners' sugar
¼   cup creamy peanut butter
¼   cup whole buttermilk

1. Preheat oven to 350°. Spray an 8x4-inch loaf pan with baking spray with flour.

2. For topping: In a large skillet, cook bacon over medium heat, stirring occasionally, until crisp, about 8 minutes. Remove bacon using a slotted spoon, and let drain on paper towels. Reserve ½ tablespoon bacon drippings.

3. In a medium bowl, whisk together flour, brown sugar, and cinnamon. Stir in melted butter and reserved ½ tablespoon bacon drippings. Stir in bacon and peanuts until crumbly; refrigerate.

4. For bread: In a large skillet, cook bacon over medium heat, stirring occasionally, until crisp, about 15 minutes. Remove bacon using a slotted spoon, and let drain on paper towels.

5. In a medium bowl, whisk together flour, baking powder, and salt. In a large bowl, whisk together mashed banana, brown sugar, melted butter, buttermilk, eggs, vanilla, and cinnamon. Stir flour mixture into banana mixture just until combined; stir in bacon and peanuts. Spread batter into prepared pan; sprinkle topping onto batter.

6. Bake for 30 minutes. Cover with foil, and bake until a wooden pick inserted in center comes out clean, about 1 hour more. Let cool in pan on a wire rack for 10 minutes. Remove from pan, and let cool completely on wire rack.

7. For glaze: In a medium bowl, whisk together confectioners' sugar, peanut butter, and buttermilk until smooth. Drizzle onto cooled bread. Store in an airtight container for up to 2 days.

BACON-STUFFED CHEESY GARLIC ROLLS

Makes 10

1 (16-ounce) package deli pizza dough
¼ cup unsalted butter, softened
1½ cups shredded sharp white Cheddar cheese, divided
1 cup crumbled cooked bacon, divided
4 tablespoons chopped fresh parsley, divided
1 tablespoon minced garlic
¼ teaspoon kosher salt
⅛ teaspoon ground black pepper

1. Spray a 10-inch cast-iron skillet with cooking spray.
2. On a lightly floured surface, roll dough into a 16x10-inch rectangle. Spread butter onto dough, leaving a 1-inch border on all sides.
3. In a small bowl, stir togther 1 cup cheese, ¾ cup bacon, 2 tablespoons parsley, garlic, salt, and pepper. Sprinkle onto dough.
4. Starting at one long side, tightly roll dough into a log; pinch seam to seal. Cut log crosswise into 10 (about ½-inch-thick) slices. Place slices, cut side up, in prepared skillet. Cover with plastic wrap, and let rise until doubled in size, about 45 minutes.
5. Preheat oven to 350°.
6. Bake, uncovered, for 18 minutes. Top with remaining ½ cup cheese and remaining ¼ cup bacon. Bake until cheese is melted, about 5 minutes more. Let cool on a wire rack for 15 minutes. Sprinkle remaining 2 tablespoons parsley onto rolls before serving.

KITCHEN TIP

If pizza dough is hard to roll out, let it stand at room temperature for 10 to 15 minutes before rolling again.

APPLE-CARAMEL CAKE WITH CANDIED BACON

CAKE

- ¾ cup unsalted butter, softened
- 1 cup firmly packed light brown sugar
- ½ cup granulated sugar
- 3 large eggs
- 1 teaspoon vanilla extract
- 3 cups all-purpose flour
- 1½ teaspoons baking powder
- ¾ teaspoon baking soda
- ¾ teaspoon kosher salt
- ¾ teaspoon apple pie spice
- 1¼ cups whole buttermilk
- 2 cups shredded peeled Golden Delicious apples

GLAZE

- 1 cup firmly packed light brown sugar
- 6 tablespoons apple cider
- 2 tablespoons unsalted butter
- 2 tablespoons bacon drippings
- 2 tablespoons dark corn syrup
- ⅛ teaspoon kosher salt
- 2 cups confectioners' sugar, sifted

TOPPING

- 4 slices thick-cut bacon
- 2 tablespoons firmly packed dark brown sugar
- ⅛ teaspoon kosher salt

1. Preheat oven to 325°. Spray a 13x9-inch baking pan with baking spray with flour.

2. For cake: In a large bowl, beat butter and sugars with a mixer at medium speed until fluffy, 3 to 4 minutes, stopping to scrape sides of bowl. Add eggs, one at a time, beating well after each addition. Beat in vanilla.

3. In another large bowl, whisk together flour, baking powder, baking soda, salt, and pie spice. With mixer on low speed, gradually add flour mixture to butter mixture alternately with buttermilk, beginning and ending with flour mixture, beating just until combined after each addition. Fold in apple. Spread batter into prepared pan.

4. Bake until a wooden pick inserted in center comes out clean, 30 to 35 minutes. Let cool on a wire rack for 15 minutes.

5. Meanwhile, for glaze: In a large saucepan, bring brown sugar, apple cider, butter, bacon drippings, corn syrup, and salt to a boil over medium heat, stirring until sugar dissolves; boil for 1 minute. Pour mixture into a large heatproof bowl.

6. Gradually add confectioners' sugar to brown sugar mixture, beating with a mixer at medium speed until mixture is smooth and begins to thicken, 2 to 3 minutes. Immediately spread glaze onto warm cake.

7. Preheat oven to 375°. Spray a wire rack with cooking spray. Place rack on a rimmed baking sheet.

8. For topping: Place bacon on prepared rack. Sprinkle brown sugar and salt onto bacon.

9. Bake until bacon is cooked through and sugar begins to dissolve, about 28 minutes. Let cool on rack until bacon is crisp. Gently remove with a spatula. Crumble bacon onto cake. Store in an airtight container for up to 2 days.

RECIPE INDEX